ON VOYAGING IN STEPHEN'S WORK

'His main subjects—seas, winds and tides, shorelines and
horizons – are expressed in precisely observed details of
shape, colour, texture and movement that capture the spirit
of a place as well as the topography in poem after poem
until voyaging becomes both fact and metaphor in Stephen's
work, a way of life and a way of interpreting life.'
—James Aitchison, *The Glasgow Herald*

ON *Adrift: New and Selected poems*, WITH PARALLEL TEXT
CZECH TRANSLATIONS

'*Adrift* offers a cross section of Ian Stephen's nearly three
decades' worth of poetic and dramatic work. His poetry
is dynamic and succinct, to the point where I have been
tempted to reproduce here, poems in their entireties.
His work has its spiritual home in the Hebrides and their
surrounding waters. For Stephen, the sea and shore are
vibrant, active; landscape is not background, it is interwoven
with the author's own personality. Stephen expresses himself
in terms alternately flowing and lyrical, or imagistic and
disaffected. He deals as readily with questions of aesthetic as
he does with the grimy trivialities of the everyday. The result
is, either way, voiced with economy and pathos.'
—Stephen Lackaye, *The Edinburgh Review*

Pittenween
Pop - up
Library

PRA

'This pursuit of the optimal way-speed was, I came to
realise, in keeping with all that Ian does. In action and
speech, he is formidably exact. He exemplifies what Robert
Lowell once called 'the grace of accuracy' and his poetry
too is distinguished by its precision. Minimalist but not
gnomic, it extends his commitments both to exactitude
and communication. There is no surfeit to it. His poems are
hort and taut as well-set sails. Poetry represents to him not
orm of suggestive vagueness, but a medium which permits
ı to to speak in ways otherwise unavailable.'

bert Macfarlane on the poetry of Ian Stephen,
· *Old Ways,* Hamish Hamilton 2012 and Penguin, 2013

VIEWS OF PUBLISHED AND BROADCAST POETRY

ılin, *Hebrides, Minches* (Dangaroo Press, Mundelstrup,
nmark, 1983)

ur poems are like washed pebbles on a beach.'
E P Thompson

ne weather feeling of the poetry is very truly matched
the photographs – altogether good lifting signals being
nsmitted…..'
Seamus Heaney, letter to Dangaroo Press

ephen writes well of the bare islanded north and its
ıscapes, its lonliness and stark, sporadic collisions with
: geopolitical and industrial-technological realities, of the
:w from the top of the world.'
-David MacDuff, *Stand* magazine

Varying States of Grace (Polygon, Edinburgh, 1989)

'Ian Stephen, a coastguard on the Isle of Lewis, has a peculiar western bravery. A number of his poems read as riskily as a high-wire act, others appear as perfectly formed exhalations. . . . . . In his robustly northern way, Stephen's eye (for he is primarily a painterly poet) is as true as his voice – careful, unobtrusive, accurate.'
—Mary Gladstone, *The Scotsman*

'He is very good on the physical world. . . . . What is there is what he writes about as if his purpose were complete in the description. Indeed his minute scrutiny is the tribute he pays to 'things' in the world.'
—Iain Crichton Smith, *The West Highland Free Press*

Providence II (The Windfall Press, Isle of Lewis, 1994)

'This beautifully produced volume of Stephen's highly individual work is drawn from the world he lives in – the seas, winds, tides, shorelines of Lewis. Stephen's poetry uses verse-forms created out of carefully controlled internal dynamics.'
—Robert Alan Jamieson, *The Edinburgh Review*

Voyagers (Radio Scotland , 1998)

'If you don't understand the lure of the sea, you haven't heard Ian Stephen explain it. Stephen writes wonderfully lyrical poetry, full of marine terminology, which he read out, to great effect, in his careful Lewis accent. But he is poetic all the time, his rhythmic voice making every syllable count, his author's insight illuminating the allure of sailing to someone who feels queasy at the sight of a mast on the horizon.'
—Anna Burnside, *The Scotsman*

maritime

new and selected poems

Ian Stephen

IMAGE AND TEXT ILLUSTRATIONS
WITH CHRISTINE MORRISON

Published by Saraband
Suite 202, 98 Woodlands Road
Glasgow, G3 6HB, Scotland
www.saraband.net

Inner typesetting and design by Gerry Cambridge
www.gerrycambridge.com

ISBN: 9781910192368

Printed in the EU on sustainably sourced paper.

The supp⟨...⟩ed is gratefully acknowledged.

CREATIVE

ALBA | CHRUTH

Cover pho⟨...⟩

1 2 3 4 5 6 7

Contents

havens

reaching out

providence

afloat and ashore

IAN STEPHEN was born in Stornoway, Isle of Lewis. He
studied education, drama and literature at Aberdeen
University then returned to live on Lewis, which remains
his home. For many years he worked for the Coastguard
Service, latterly managing a watch. He resigned in 1995 on
winning the inaugural Robert Louis Stevenson award and
has worked full-time in the arts since then. His novel,
A Book of Death and Fish, was published by Saraband in 2014.

Poems from his first collection, *Malin, Hebrides, Minches*
were set to music (Diethelm Zuckmantel) and performed
in Dusseldorf. A St Kilda libretto, devised with the
composer David P Graham, was performed in Bonn and
Cologne and later published in Berlin. The British Council
funded the translation of a previous volume of poems into
Czech. Other poems were his response to the Festival of
Island Literature in Ouessant, Brittany. Stephen has also
represented Scotland in a translation project, linking
the Scottish Islands to the Mediterranean. He was a guest
at the Edmonton Poetry Festival, Alberta as part of the
2014 Commonwealth Poets United project and at the
Australian Wooden Boat Festival, Tasmania, in 2015.

This collection concentrates on the maritime strands in
his work. Poems from previous collections are often
in a new version and not always in chronological order.

THIS BOOK IS DEDICATED TO ANGUS DUNN,
POET AND MAKER OF STORIES, ALWAYS
Looking for the Spark

AND TO ALEXANDER HUTCHISON, POET —
HIS ENERGY, CARING AND ZEST FOR OUR SHARED
CURRENCY OF WORDS IS PRESENT IN
Bones and Breath

havens

Cotton kept by the boiled bark of oaks.

Red lead

My present standpoint makes way.
Able seamen stab at rust.
I'll go for specific orange,
locally in its place as
a temporary stop
of singing oxide.

I bide within limited parallels.
Shuffle a few meridians.
Too much point or too much span
fail to fix a position
on the bend of a globe.

Elegies are all about.
I'm for red lead.
A brush with poison
startling against decay.

Under the pier

It was a green world we went in, under the pier.
Up there, above, the dockers caught ropes
and metal boxes that had been tied to lorries
swung over the pier with vegetables and fridges
and wool and chocolate biscuits.

We never walked when we went under but
chased a way down ladders of weedy metal
and then we leaped but no-one ever
fell in, that we remember.

It would have been a disgrace, that,
if anyone's slip of a sandshoe had sent them
to splash the greenness into wetness.
We would have been surprised – halted
the game surely and then swapped looks
copied from schoolteachers, ones that said,
'I'm disappointed in you.'

Nickname

Thinking of when you brought home
that Che Guevara teeshirt.
It gave you your nickname –
the short Che lengthened
with our local vowel.

When the batteries ran out
and rock ceased to roam with us
on Sunday streets and tracks,
while your parents were driving
you made the omelettes,
adding drips of water
to crisp the edges.

When everything creative
was in your scullery –
hard lead softening
on the hotplate.
Our clay moulds shaped
with fingers and thumbs.

The good grace in
our fumbling years –
when we threw sinkers
with trailing barbs
to take red rock cod.

Meeting up – poems for James

1. *Race* (June 1972)

A defined heel,
out of sand spray.
Your nose out front
then lagging to
the small surf.
We were more or less
abreast till
my inspired ankle
crossed space
to drive your trailing heel
against your leading leg.

You spilled
with splayed hands.
I fell over you.
It beat school.

2. *Meeting* (January 1994)

You named the rendezvous.
I waited between lions,
drifted round to the shut main gates
till you led us away from the museum
to a King's Cross lock-in club
furnished with vinyl and Caribbean and
Hebridean islanders abroad.

I lost the helm completely.
The wheel spun with splintering handles.
The glasses piled
but we weren't as lost
as the kids outside.

On watch

To my west I see
a starboard green lamp,
a white on the mast,
one lit wheelhouse
above the calm black
and a blurred inversion.

To my east, the radio
transmits something like
what it received.
Internal action in Poland –
tanks mobilised
over cut wires.

Here and now is recognition
of our harbour approaches
in all states of tides
and the sensing of pale
liver in slit
mottled flanks
of cod and ling.

Halibut

In the lee of Holm Island
he hauled five stones of halibut.
It surfaced on a single snood.

        where the pelagic fishers now
        pair-trawl from steel hulls
        pursuing soundings

He sold it to be sold again
– a tin roof on brick walls
where the weather-cock was a fish.

        where the vehicle park is now
        crowded or desolate
        according to schedule

He tells me how he towed the thing,
still writhing on the gaff,
towards buyers with their brassy names.

        now I know they're wide abeam—
        our bow-waves and stern-wakes,
        his memory, my empathy

Baptist church (abandoned)

Corner-stones, scree
and sunk lintels,
close to the cliff.

Shaped long gaps
in one remaining wall
look to the east.

Some congregation
either went adrift
or further afield.

May Hiortaçh

May Hiortach once said
she'd go back tomorrow or before
if the roof was put on number three.
Tar or thatch, pitch or tin.
Hirta was the inhabited place at
the edge of the lesser Atlantic fathoms
before the drop.

May lived next door to us, in the cul-de-sac
at sixty-four Kennedy Terrace.
She seemed settled.

Hiortach – a person from *Hiort* or Hirta, St Kilda

Old boat

We touched the transom.
We couldn't see
Bayble island.

There was no wind.
The stern was still.
The boat, shored,

lay calm in
flaked paint.
Wood sores
bared to haar.

Too cold to sleep,
we floated dry
miles from noise.

Shiants

The basking islands
like sails, fins, teeth.

High wings of black blades
as the barnacle geese pass.

The blue men of narrations are
the grey seals, treading water.

Our cleated and welted movements go
by beaked clowns, lambing ewes.

Shiant shepherds

A calm below teeming airspace.
A task for a flight-controller —
steering the routes of razorbills,
puffins and ripple-breasting shag.

Gear stored in fertiliser-sacks,
strung with one sheep, three dogs.
Men, beasts and gas bottles
come across to us.

These five ordinary souls
worked out their weeks on the Shiants
on turf-padded rocks, mid-Minches
while their climber ewes had their lambs.

They wear their eccentricities
in their tammies and bonnets but
these men with the calm in their bellies
lived somewhere obscured to ourselves.

Scarp Island

Walking through wetness,
denim drying on skin.
A drifted marker,

stranded, redundant. It
could be from the *Strachans*.
She still works the great-lines.

I can't make out the sequence
in fixed-wing gyrations
of the aerial colony.

On sphagnum and moss
a convoluted root
is bent over forwards.

How many families lived
by the seaweed kilns
in the iodine reek?

Three lyrics

1.

Look wider than the broadest bay
but give me blue of mussel shell
and yellow of the winter sky.

Salt and liquor
on our tongues.
Give and keep
that mollusc blue.

2.

Burn mouth bleeds to minor delta
out to slow and drowning flanks.
Unlikely green sets through reds —
smaller stream to larger sea.

Herring-oiled and flatcalmed patches
three waves, five and half a mile out
still the swimming
take the weight,
return you
light as a shell
to sand.

3.

Should we plant a rowan here
at the sea-loch side?
The seed of red berries
for imagination,
to germinate
in this day
when leaves mould
and stars die.

A hawthorn for healing,
spur and leaf balm.
Rooting for
the pair of us
and for us all.

Kinloch Resort

Did you dwell here with me
in this beehive of placed stones,
put there for the summers
when the cattle were heavy?

Did our barley rigs hold
in deep cleared furrows
between the acidic
and the salted rocks?

Did you bait the lines, here
at the head of this steep loch
where Sron Ulladale bears
to the whitefish grounds?

We should make a fire now.
Pile it this ebb tide
to the high water strewing
of packets and canisters.

Bridge at Ardroil

The surface of larch is bleached.
The heart of the rail is stable.

Timber content with its moisture.

Lagoon

from a photo by Scott Murray

One bare backbone lies
white on saithe-green grass
– the signature of
a huddled heron.

Thrush by water

There's no disturbance
of my ripples
by tappings
even when I see
the source is
breaking shells
anvilled by a thrush.

The picturesque sound
by wave-lap is
the death of snails.
Sifting and tapping
without discord.
No jarring changes
come to sound.

reaching out

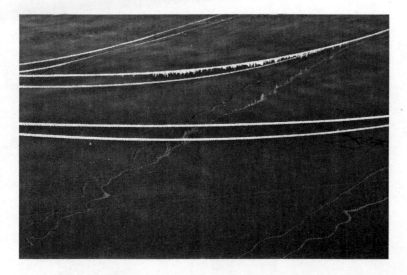

A running mooring is an endless loop.

Sanday

Expansive skies
as in Dutch masters
but these are faster —
shifting light tones.

Sea colours assault
both shores and eyes.
A lot of angry white
breaking from brilliance.

Dry dykes could never
hold that water out
so grazings and furrows
are backspaced
a field-fathom

but lichened slabs,
cemented just high enough
to make muted roofs,
stay put
on built frames.

Gales ruffle skins
of sand and walls,
of cattle and dwellings
and pass over all.

Wyre to Rousay

for Rosie, after Edwin Muir

We did not know why it was strange
to circumambulate Wyre.
Tripping rubber over slate-slabs
and rounding piles of convex stones.
The piping terns. The still skuas.

The ferry then lifted us across
to let us touch the Rousay shore.
We took the contour past tilled ground
to the smooth curve of once-sown grass —
a form on a chambered cairn.

We lay on top of old and new,
resting on the circumference
of that protected monument,
to view the extent of Wyre's length,
shin-bone like, stretched, but

scraped with some living ribs of fields
and the lesser bones of rafters
left behind a partial exodus.
Some went further overseas than us.
We linger here, with our eyes.

St Malo

The swamped concrete platforms
by the silted pools. Elvers
entering with the red moon tide.

Hitchcock lightning or maybe Chabrol,
threatening the ramparts, the keep and
slighting our sea-wood fire.

Sanctuary

Nets strung like hammocks and Paul Strand slats
on a jetty by Giacometti.
The blocks won't run, spars won't work.

Above all this balanced decay
a high lark sends out its beacon
into an inexplicable haze.

Over a snake of blown polythene,
one drifting magpie, one planing harrier
patrol the blockade of marram grass

and sea-kale that binds the dunes
before a wet mudflat desert —
this exposed sanctuary.

Estuary, Bayonne

The forked kite-tail, the
finely tuned wings, like
a long and lean cruising kestrel
methodical hunger over
the drowned maple leaf and
the swimming artichoke while

a man on a moped goes
in varying states of grace
along the busy banking with
his bundle of the sections of
his dismantled mullet-pole,
longer than his machine.

Poems for BZ

1. *Arnish*

Kippers on your breath and
the washed smell of your hair.

The war memorial on the tower.
The Arnish light and its beacon –

that was once a reflective mark
broadcasting the light received.

Your own course, not yet set.
Your green and disarming eyes.

Tension of leeway and keel
in the tracings of our wakes.

2. *Afloat, die Alster*

The sound of wet comes from underneath.
A knotted painter brings the boat's stride
up short and it needs a conscious arm
to stop the jolt against the mooring.

We laugh in the clumsy shape.
We're not upon the North Sea.
A single sternward oar-cut

for small sculling
to some sort of work
in this lake that is an island in
various degrees of city light.
I say we are like sixteen-year-olds on
a Friday night. We don't want to go home.

But your irregular sway is stronger,
'Sometime we must make a baby in a boat.'

3. *Elbe*

Nolde skies and waters on the Elbe.
International buoyage and the washes
of tanker, coaster and riverboat seeming
greater between these limits of width.

Delays till their wakes hit the banks
and shudder the empty caravan park
where small fertilities of shrubs
mark the claims of next season.

Ship-diesels shunt and somewhere are
hammering propellers. Sea-couplings.

4. *Rackwick Bay*

Your boots are inert and laces blur
like all other lines. The only movement
on this shore is in folds and veins.

A moaning boom sounds out to all
from lingering breeze in cliff-caves.
A power of light penetrates haar
while someone, under a fore-cuddy,
fishes the drift off St John's Head.

We're surely not the first to need to lie
heavily here, open to
the dominance of sound
and slower sympathetic sense.

5. *Stromness*

Green and red are chained to calm
in this harbour, warm as rum and
I've lost my reciprocal
bearing to your track and
want to make good
my late reach home.

6. *At Luskentyre*

Your salt-clogged hair
is rippled like
long abrasions
in sea sand.

I take you all in
and trust that threats,
overhead or undersea,
will remain remote
or be quietened
like the hard blue lines
grown hairy in
this range of tides.

7. *Mooring*

I'm lying with you a mile inland
under rain that drills the roof-sheets
and storms all chinks in the flashings.
The sealed window-unit isn't.
The peats, still out, are wasting in wet.
Sean and Ben are sound, along the ridge.

There happens to be a power-cut
and there's a depth of singing height
above the weather — but we're not
moored to anything I've seen
sink or rise on a tested line.
We'll hold together tonight.

At Plockton

In the ebb of pleasure here,
embedded in pebbles,
like the keel, settled for winter,
anchored by a welter
of orange lines.

The continuing causes
sore as
Spain or Ireland.
Present life is tense.
Water stills before the boil
leaving me cold and
out of season
in the knuckle of
this promontory.

The poet Sorley MacLean was a school teacher in Plockton. Like
Auden, he weighed the passions of the moment against the shock-
waves, emanating across Europe from the Spanish Civil War.

The amber shores of Rugen Island

It doesn't have to be like anything else —
red rags frapping on
a beached black quarter,
elegant yellow of stressed jibs
shifting blocks on Baltic skylines.

Small seas on random rubble.
An easy breathing.
Collapsing dunes, punctuated
with dispersed pine-trunks.

It doesn't have to be like anything else —
the folded memory of paint systems,
a dull engulfing of harl and dash,
endpapers glued to standing gables.

We read the architecture.
A safe classical circus in Putbus.
Fisher-row thatches dodge the snap
of gusting over Gohren headland.
Finnish knowhow
in the Party highheidyins' Cliff Hotel.

A gradual sifting of iron leakage
in waters heavy with suspended chalk.
These slow-shifting cliffs don't
have to be like vanilla but they are.
Caspar David Friedrich was here.

Beech stems on clifftops
don't have to suggest
Paul Nash. But they do.
Zeppelin skies gave way
to Stukas and Migs.
Lockheed Starfighters
dropped down dead.

Eyes back down to tentacle tips.
You'd need a diamond to drill them now.
Sifting through losses and victories.

This moon is in her first quarter,
a phase into another last year
but strong enough to compete
with neon from the redeveloped pier.

Here the fronts come over forests
or else they traverse open water.
Slight rise and fall.
No short alliances
of tidal stream and actual breeze.
No squalling
oppositions.

Photographer unknown

A Fin Whale on the 'O plain' at Crytoiken, South Georgia, 2 March 1935

Gelatin trapped the silver
that ran through the fingers
of the men in high seaboots.

Calum or Angus
on the flensing knife
for as long as the print is fixed
under the high white hills
of Crytoiken

which could be
West Loch Tarbert
in Lord Leverhulme's dream,
exposed in
some Sunlight land.

Lord Leverhulme: founder of Lever Brothers (Sunlight Soap) —
a philanthropic entrepreneur who, as proprietor of Lewis
and Harris, pursued several doomed projects including
a whaling station at West Loch Tarbert.

Albertac *a photograph by Beken of Cowes*

for Colin and Barbara Myers

She's cleared the gable
at the head of a pier,
left the piles, the lanterns,
bricks, derricks. Out to
the sediment of Essex
as the men hold on to their wires
as the officers only have to adjust
the angles of unlikely hats.

All that stuff, pretty and practical,
is detritus or treasure now.
It could be carbon in a burned boatyard
or heirlooms on mantelpieces
– salvaged members.

My dead friend Norman said
the bulb that started an exposure
was like the gut of a herring,
maybe like a scrotum.
So light is lent like milt.

Norman Malcolm Macdonald in his play *The Shutter Falls*
and in his novel, *Portrona* (Polygon, 2000).

Clyde coast

Is it all about shine?
An insane degree of care
in the brightwork of a fleet for hire
on the dinky side-slip,
reflecting back the light
bounced down from Nardini's.
Silver in all the elegant vinyl names
though one does say
White Heather.

A banjo man in a back room
has the wrinkled pride of Alan Breck.
He shows his teeth when
the strings shine
ahead of any conscious plan.
Pete Seeger's name is dropped
into the dustbowl grizzle of his beard.
Nothing idle, there.

Down the road in Ayr
an engineer has retired
to frazzle sausages
and relate his solutions
to hydraulic issues
for the National Opera's *Billy Budd.*
They gave him drawings.
He made the kit.
His voice is luminous
as the perfect yolk.

Now on the twice-missed Rothesay ferry,
there's a man in a scarlet fleece
combing the hair of a woman
in a vermilion showerproof coat.
They stand in borrowed light.
They shine.

Piper in the city

If it's a march it's a slow one.
Absent comrades, folk
not really managing

as the boy blows the rain from his reed
and the shoppers go for it,
the pace of Sauchiehall Street
over the echoes
of rebounding swell.

It was just down the Clyde,
Bowling to Rothesay.
We berthed to catch
the one late pint.
Asking for a guy
I now know is dead.

A teacher, a good one.
He could talk to his pupils.
Quite a young man.
I don't know the story.

The march doesn't need one.
Something that moves you
all the more
in its labouring.

The Buddhist buoys of Pittenweem

The Buddhist buoys
of Pittenweem,
frap blue flags
on breaking white.

Their bobbing line
marks a contour
along to the breakwater.

A red pumping
port hand light
steers you in close.

Donmouth (circa 1965)

I find it amongst the
varnished octagonals
of Sharpe's split canes.
A cheap glass rod
to cast Swedish spinners
back towards the Baltic.

At a spit
at Donmouth
the flare of tinsel
escaping bindings.
There will be a steel wreck soon.
but it's not yet grounded
at the navigable limit of surf.

And back home west
the concrete beacon
on the east tip of Arnish reef
(Approaches to Stornoway)
has not fallen down yet.
But it will.

Sure as the Caley Hotel
at our seafront
will go on fire
with loss of life.
That's history but
these things
have not happened yet.

I hope there's a trout for me,
dense speckles,
black on silver,
migrating in
but the other guys
lob worms
to the bottom

for flounders who shift their eyes
to the tops of their heads.
Their own rough ridges
showing through
the tidal solutions
for those who can see.

In the Royal Museum of Scotland

for Barolong Seboni

The blue whale of Portobello
stretches under the balcony.
Its industrial jaws
show their mechanism
but you have to imagine
a delicate corset
of slatted baleen.

The spinal links are numbered
but you know they supported
a body with limitless range
till it stranded.

A speaking comes from under it –
the voice of a Botswanian friend,
met at The Meadows the night before.
'You can have that one, island man.'

A level below,
he pats the preserved elephant.
'This is my ship but
it's not how I'm going home.'

A night-fishing

W S Graham, David Hume Tower,
Edinburgh University

Rips and surges
drove under the doors
of the glazed tower.

Our deck of laminates
lifted. The parquet
buckled to waves.

I don't think he could
make good
the course of his lines.

It was a Mayday —
'emotion or heartburn'
he said to his chest
from under his heavy hair.

He lost his plot
but swayed on.
I couldn't grasp a theme
but I got his drift.

providence

Older pencil marks on charts used for previous passages.

Seilebost

Our island is discontent as light
glancing under precipitation –
a weather system from south of Islay.
Ireland is there, under Malin Head.

A melting landmass in the dunes of
Seilebost. Toe Head is out as an arm
but insufficient to shield the machair.

Then there are the katabatic bursts of breeze
against the grain of decent predictions
bringing destroying brightness

to brush down deep
below the several surfaces
of the Sound of Taransay.
Constant as change.

Boat-burning

In terms of light, it's the longest day.
Oystercatchers are even crazier
than ever or since the last time I was here

by dried-out marine-ply
shedding greens and greys. Skelfs
breaking free from primers.

I strain to see more than
what's visible in tones
that lie between the

timber block and the
charcoal it's becoming.
Loud colour in
a stench of flame.

Repairs and maintenance

It seems to nearly matter what the wind is doing
across the tidal mess I've learned to live with.
There's an intimation of
a backing breeze to carry sleet.

Some have no other option but
to put to sea with unspectacular resolve
and gamble with the fuel bill
or face the bank.

The costs are certain, against
whatever's dragged up
from 'The Roundabout'
plumbed into Decca.

Saleable tails
broken from
luminous spines.

You still have a sort of choice
when it's not your living
and a lot of buckshee expert help.

Take the problem of the ribs —
sawn true to a snug template
placed on the lap of planks,
or bent hot from oak straps
steamed to tendons.

Variables

Roddy's boat is a Faroese yole
— nineteen foot that won't go metric.
Matt and resin, moulded
to pine lines.

She takes, bow on,
a filling swell that
rises like cumulus.

Her silvered engine shakes its bracket
with a slightly steadier temperament than
the petrol-paraffin combination job
which usually got us far enough
to drop soft mussel
to whiting mouths.

There's healing out there yet
in the recurrence of variable conditions
even though the leather sponsons
of St Brendan's new boat
bumped bits of oil,
crude and clotted.

Landfill

Bait-gathering with the tide down.
I scour the rocks on Sober Island
and remember a rusty Spaniard

tied up at Number One. Crew diving
from uneven rails, brown bodies
bursting a lubricant sheen.

We traded mackerel for bags of wine
and went home brave in sour red
to inquiring glances.

But we were keen to gut, boil and eat
whitefish caught off Sgeir Mhor
downtide from the outfall pipe.

Now I wouldn't eat fish or bivalve
caught in Approaches to Stornoway
but my waste goes to Beinn na Drobha,

a site hidden from the sea,
nestled beneath landmarks I need
and out of mind like domestic debris

and like the high-security cans
from Dounreay or Sellafield
drowned or buried in wet or dry

insensitive areas.
Now you see them.
Now you don't.

Providence

Venture, Fear Not, Providence 2.
Our first glass hull is frayed.

Moraldie is now a *White Rose.*
The red, the green, the purple.

Astra, Forgiveness, Diana 2.
Gloss weeps rust.

On the Shiant Banks
colours and numbers.

We find the plot
on a flickering screen.

The *Wave Crest* is on the slip.
Her lettering is touched.

Coastguarding

1. Return to Lochinver

So this is the place
the franked wood boxes
should be returned to.

Soyea and her outlying skerries
have broken these incoming seas.
From here we only see the effects

under the fog which survives
a southwesterly five.
All these recurring names

along the seaboard we guard.
The first position we received
for the grounded Loch Erisort

was inside Soyea Island.
A red flare reported
on the 999.

No contact on the VHF.
We pencilled on the charts.
Sent the lifeboat and the cruiser.

Put out the updates
to the Minch
in the relays.

Each vessel recovered
the remains of one man.
The rest was up to the telex.

Address lists on tape.
Carriage returns.
Line spaces.

A log of times
for the Inquiry.

2. *I'll boil the kettle*

I'll boil the kettle since the mainlight's on,
breaking areas of anglepoise arcs
on colour-coded panels of contacts.

The skipper of the *Golden Sheaf* can
pass the tow in sheltered water –
'Over to you, Calum, at Loch Sealg.
The bacon and eggs are on, below
and I'd better see about catching a crust
to share between the boys on Friday.'

That job is set against the residue
of another task, up the latitude.
Clear of the Butt and at eight degrees west.
A crewman simply went over the rails.
He jumped out to the calm night.
They threw fluorescence, dropped a boat.

We sent a chopper with potent spans
of live lights. It only found
a brash litany
of flotation devices.

3. *Fatal Accident Inquiry*

Bracelets of small stuff
failed to support them.

Frayed fibre strands
teased out
in orange and blue
on yellow cuffs
sticking like
a charge of neglect

but this evidence
is mute
and no-one can tell us
if these dumb lashings
were a standard protection
from daily runs of drips

or a last-gasp measure,
tied-in fast
to capture air
in smocks of PVC
as the hull began a slide
she'd not come back from.

The quiet crises
must have begun
like any small snag –
three strands biting
sweating steel
on the running hauler.

A trap meant for crabs,
down below,
fastened as
the swell rose on
and the vessel did not.

The sea released them
a fortnight later
when pressure relented.

'All that could have been done...
was done.'
But you still relive
every call.

4. *Night watch*

The night watch is slanted
in anglepoise light
away from the obvious.
The *Girl Lauren* calls.
She's dodging off the Kebock.
'It's a poor night.

It's the clutch.
If we get her jammed in gear
we'll go for Ullapool.
No, we're not making much of it.
Most likely make for Stornoway now.
It's a very poor night here.'

Our cream barograph settles low.
Tide is bumped above our tables.
The *Suilven* floats, open-mouthed
above the linkspan.
Police close The Peninsula.

The stranded drivers must be blinking as
the Shiants are set in place by light.
This time the seas go back.
Shed tails of kelp are left
on the tarmac of the isthmus.

Lesson

conversation with Astie

He'd had enough of the logic of circuits.
Fished, mended, steered.
Spun his meshes round the frames.
Mended fathoms and fathoms of trawl.

Took the bearings for his ticket.
Faced up to the oral exam.
Only caught a body once but
strange things surfaced in the cod-end.
A mine. The carcass of a heifer.

Catriona getting us tea and loaf.
Our fingers taking up our spikes.
The lay of the rope, the order of tucks.

Three strand is easy.
You have to pick the one in the middle.
Then you start with the one below it.
But see that last one. Bend it back
all the long way round to its place.

Tension the strands back on themselves.
Risk suited him more than routine.
That's what it came to, net gain.

The Bo

There's still a ling to be had on the Bo.
You're over it when the boulder's open
on the breast up from the red rock
and the war-memorial is in line
with the middle turret of the castle.

Grunting gurnard and beady-eyed conger
scarce now as religious haddock
which used to shoal on lugworm mud.
But there's a small colony of ling
on this Bo that snares trawls,
takes hooks and anchors
into her kelp.

Our plummeting small-line has broken sea
and pulls down the paid-out sequence
of spade-end hooks on snoods

softer to the touch than the braided brown.
Our washing-line of cuts of bait
sacrificed from the shaking shoulder
of a tense mackerel.

The lively swivel.
The end-stop weight
to blue riser to
the daft pink
of the floating puta.

Ling, with cod-marblings and barbel but
with their fullness elongated like eel,
take a better price on West Coast floors

than all save
lemons and monks. But
we're not asking for a box, only

one to take home to scoff with the olman.
One for Kenny who gave us the deck-paint.
One for Audy who cast us his line.

Bo (from the Gaelic word *bogha*)   a submerged reef, but
   the Bo in Stornoway refers to a specific mark, off the
   Arnish Moor shoreline;
puta   one of several Gaelic words for a buoy, imported into
   Stornoway usage;
olman   father

Recreation

I'm gasping at the gills with fish
swimming in beer and vinegar.
Men, even modern ones you say,
are a disgrace when they're pissed
on rum and heavy and reminiscence.
I want to loiter by bollards
and the rest of the surviving
archaeology of recreation –
going to sea in angling boats with
reels made in Redditch or Japan.

There's more than salt sediment
crystals on a double bloodknot,
more than recorded pounds,
ounces and drams as well.
There's an unsteady sort of love
for those who saw me as the apprentice
and that is as reliable in its way
as your own steadiness now
steering me up the road home
and we're not, you say,
setting any alarm
for any morning tide.

Peace and Plenty

Up to my neck in blue,
the channel-island gensey
of a dead Maciver.
The garment imported
with the word for it.

Darned cuffs and collar
exerting nothing
– slack sailcloth.
But the rib knit
holds me.
My share.
He gave me it
while he could see it on me.

Audy believed in sharing,
providing Security
over the Department's counter.
Under it, if he had to.

The marks I pass to crews are his.
His herring, his thornback
come over my bulwarks.
Like that son of a tailor
I've escaped in a skiff,
returned to tell the story –

cracking frost,
steel to mussel,
the tugs of bites.

Distributing
the flapping
whitings.

Two Cemeteries

I haven't patience for the clouds,
spectacular enough today
from Kebock Head to Arnish Point.
Strange how your eyes settle for detail
under this longstone lintel.
Trapped deer's heads, stone bones,
the bulge of flesh in a relief
of some MacLeod lying in state.

Out the walls, into the westerly,
I want to be content with glimpses
of a sunny and storm-blown fankle:
driftrope captured on a groyne
at the fatted limit of tide
but my mind is driving on the tar
that's laid out towards my town
and a burial ground in better repair.

Looking across the draped urns,
through the iron basket beacon
that stands on Sgeir Mhor and bears
to derricks breaking sky at Glumaig,
I can't avoid a foreground stone
in marble we all chose from the catalogue –
'A Devoted Wife And Mother'.

Gilt is sneaked upon by moss.
Why did she
have to live through us?

Two navigators

for Alma Gregory

You lost your own airman,
gone missing over Germany.
You found your way, surface,
to this other Long Island.

You came to wear
Harris wool,
the oil and hues
of this unrealistic place
where warmth and condemnation
walk with linked arms
to share mutton
after the sermon.

Your paced drawl,
a gentle discord
with the Gaelic vowels
in our English.

I think of you now
at our airfield
while Nissan huts oxidise,
their sheeting still curved tight
against low weather.

Transatlantic spirits
huddle in horsehide
by the shells of their Ansons.

Paraffin is faint
over salt rushes.

Side-ward

John is in pale sky-blue.
James in Paisley patterns.

John has his mission –
to shed a layer so
he can lie in nothing but his pad.
Bend his legs. Sense cool.

James goes with the drip.
Flickers to his daughter's Gaelic.

'He was in the convoys you know.
Came back to shore in a lifeboat.
They'd all been given up for lost.
He only spoke about it recently.'

We talk across
the one room and
the men in pyjamas.

'To listen to John
World War II was all about
a stolen sack of almonds.
A feast of geese.'

My father catches his name.
He gives us the thumbs up.

But the desolate ocean is
as close as their
infected breath.

afloat and ashore

Moments of clear watchkeeping and the dripping hours.

Shipping Forecast

You talk to me over
wearing water.
You're ashore,
I'm afloat

on carvel, clinker,
trenails, rivets
welds, ply or
2-part epoxy.

All protecting
as far as able.

A grammar of wavelength

with the Inshore Fishing Community of Mull and Iona

1. Dawn Treader

You don't want too much yellow an red.
Going to the hard. That packed sand.
They can be there and all but.
Fancy wee buggers.
Need to be.
I been at them twenty-odd year.

Gardner. Whale. Spencer-Carter.
Eminox. Besto Buoy.

You couldn't tube them up in the North.
Hell o a short shite o a sea.
A high jabble.

White Post. Ardtornish. Ben Eileanan.
Garmony Point. Sgeir nan Gobhar. Scallastle Bay.

Squatties – hellova futtery beasts.
Fasteners – creels that come up
too damn fast.
Aye launch it Donald.

These'll count 8 or 9
to the 2 pound.

Good prawns, these.
Maybe they'll last us
through September.
October, the velvets.
Lynn of Lorne.

2. Western Belle

Too big to work in
wee corners,
she's 26 metres.
Western Belle.

Used to be
more boats towing
less dredges.

Looking for shell
or going to a peak.
Coming off it a bit.
Trying to work round it.
All in Decca.
Red and purple.

Now it's the colours of your track.
Exact edges of the ground.

The gear's the same.
Bellies last
eighty days

when you're dredging
24 hours
ten a side
at £90 each.
The swords last
two to five days
at £11 each
in abrasive ground.

3. *Out of Ulva Ferry*

a.

That's the Dutchman's Cap.
Lunga and the Carn na Burghs.
Sometimes light hits on Coll.
Houses float in flat sea.

The track is centred on the GPS.
You can shift it to read in Decca for
your paper charts. Just about
get it to put the tea on.

MacQuarrie's rock jumps
from 30 fathoms to that.
I wouldn't worry but.
It's got a kind of rounded top —
been hit that often.

Leave the first skerry tight to port
the second to starboard and
line the yellow pole on
the painted block of white.

b.

Hard sand and cobbles.
Gear's lying north to south.
We shoot east to west – but
they've swung right round in the gale.
Seventeen days down,
they might be bunching.
Hasn't been any weather in it.
That sharp wedge is Lunga.
A flat line'll draw Tiree.

No gale or strong wind warning in force.
Local navigational warning, Skye Bridge Area.
Wiskey Zulu one eight seven nine.

The more the echoes
the harder the ground.

c.

From the southeast they come in threes.
Standing right up, whatever's around them.
You see them coming.
It doesn't help you.

Holding the cage. Cage in the water.
If she rolls back you'll get the next one.
If you're still afloat you'll cope with the third.

4. Anzac

Looks like a scrapyard
till you see it happening.
It's all over the side and
there's your working decks.

At 10 or 12 metres
give or take overhangs
you're getting hard transmission
through the deck.
Basically
in grand contact.

Much beyond that and
you're an android.
You've done the damage and
don't know it till
it's on the surface.

It's got to be steel.
Big sheets in the chines.
Coupla long seams
welded so you don't
dislocate and
you'd swear it was
a round bilge.

Forward looking sonar.
The radar for the fog.
The two GPSs
linked to the plotter.
Liquid crystal
flat, compact.

Four options for
the depth under you.
Feet fathoms metres
and something called
passa brassa
on the Furuno.

5. *Dubh Artach*

A broad band of red
round grey Dubh Artach.

Stephen's dad was stationed there.
CLIPPER SEAFOODS.
Stevenson's dad built it.
We move around a lot.

BRADAN LIMITED
So do the crabs,
faster than you'd think.

Sometimes it's hard
MARINE HARVEST
to be a woman

Out of the speakers.
Last boat was glass
DUN EOCHALLA
– slower but she served us well.

International Orange
flecks the indigo
of the lobsters.

Ruby are you contemplating
SEATRADE
going out somewhere.

Series from *inshore* (pink and black), *an Tobar*, Isle of Mull
recorded with Gordon Maclean and Jack Evans at *an Tobar*
exhibition, performance and publication with Celtic Connections.

Tracking

We record the tracking
of a vessel underway
as a legal requirement.
Our logs are kept
for safety's sake but
some passages
are exposed
and fixed.

Log – a record of your way through water

for Gavin Wallace and Brian Johnstone who made this happen

1. *Leaving Stornoway*

It's a dirty big equinoctial ebb.
You wrote how our mud smells –
'Seven centuries of herring guts.' *

The backcombed incoming sea
looks like joined up whitings –
a jostle in the pan of the hoil.

Thinking of your own
Zulu fishermen
looking down to the shoals,
'maroon' in the 'indigo' –

the colour scheme of a Broad Bay boat,
the *Hope* of Angie Wheems.

* from *Portrona*, a community play and novel by Norman
  Malcolm Macdonald
hoil   the Stornoway word for harbour

2. *Southeasterly gale, Stromness*

There's a fair bit of east in it still.
The laziest wind, as they say,
doesn't bother to go round you,
just goes straight through.

And the gentle men at the harbour
warped our own white horse, last night,
pretty wild on the rope,
out of the teeth of it all
while we slept ashore.

The kind of day they open the low door,
the warming oven of the Rayburn.
Invite you to cast aside the boots
and stick your woollen feet in.
Your nose in the steam of a browning scone
done on the plate like slate on the top.

If it's about anything, it's about this —
visiting relations, out of town,
the watch-mates met again
in The Ferry Inn or on
the bridge of the *Hebrides*.

The way one phrase nudges another.
The history of your way through weather.
The chat of your people.

3. Skara Brae

A run ashore

Anne's office is perched at the site.
The filing cabinets face the door.
It opens to winds that used to prevail.
That reef, the building bar of stones,
is extending out, she says,
'like the bay is looking after itself'.

4. Bring Deeps

Stromness to Burray, on El Vigo

Power up the main to clear the red.
Plotting set. We'll need to tack now.
Steer to clear that Rysa Little.

Eyes off the soundings on the chart,
to study the very shapes of shallows,
stramash around lines of eddy.

That's Cava. The Barrel of Butter.
Now we can use
the full bight
of Da Flau.

5. Session

The fiddle's chattering to the cauld wind
pipes and John's bass kicks.
Kitty and Norman's boxes
squeeze and shunt
the vectors of the session.
Cooking on gasoline.
It's all bending fine.

The boat's moored in
whatever breeze.
Lines of only maybe arrivals
smudge in the backspray of
the jabble that shines out and up
to visibility, moderate or poor.

Today, the sight of height
was only an idea of
the hidden hills of Hoy.

Forecast of severe gales from the south. *El Vigo* moored
at Water Sound, Burray.
Journey by ferry and bus to join *Reaper* on voyage from
Anstruther to St Andrews.

6. *Anstruther to St Andrew's Bay*

Aboard Reaper. *For Tam and Ian*

Git that bonnet in your pocket.
You're on the east coast noo.
The green's nae a colour for luck.

      A long black ship turns tight stone corners,
      a postie's jig on sympathetic warps
      and the full keel's clear, we're on the road.

We'd gang intil Stornoway, on to Faroes.
A spoke or twa roond 215 ill dae for noo.
See that marker. If you're doon this way,
three tides meetin. Keep a clearance.

      I'm seeing a shading in tones of water,
      the bounce of light from incidental land
      observed along this sea-road trip –
      double Suilven, Baltic Orkney and
      the soft and stubborn haar of Fife.

A ba hair margin. All we're wantin.

      The bend and slide
      of the whole tune
      easy as Tam
      as he sneaks her through
      St Andrew's lock.

7. *Stromness to Stornoway*

Return in El Vigo

They say you want to look a beast in the eye
but see these grumpy ones, come a long way,
I'm not so sure it helps to look behind
and they're usually just playful
scratching their long backs
on your passing keel.
A hiss of steam and on they go
to where they're bound.

Then there's the sloppy ones,
always in threes, the Mull guys say,
when the pressure's been high and
there's a strong and dry southeasterly.
They don't mean to make a menace of themselves.
They're more curious like as one of them breaks
with a slap on your shoulder, into the cockpit.
Maybe another rough greeting,
just to catch the craic of your ship.
You listen out for the next.

From *It's About This* — a log of an attempt to sail *El Vigo* to
StAnza festival, 2004.

At the herring

At the herring this year
in the September dips
to near-dark –
the sky of skate wings
in black butter.

Exemouth

for Graham Rich and Lesley Kerman

A tumble of channel sea
is steered to the shallow and narrow
then let go, churning, like
butter at its burning point.

A steadier white ridge,
a gap and higher strata
in the joined movement of birds.

The bar is exposed to October.
Like the skin of a shark,
it waits for wet.

Temperature dips.
Colour diminishes
to the white of one egret
the grey of eight herons.

Dull red falls
to its form in the rushes.

Ebb tide, Exemouth

The fall of the bow
till
prop blades show
and the lateral line
isn't
but the crabber is still
as reeds nod.

That's what happens
but it's a bit different
this and every
ebb and flood.

Long Seas

from St Kilda Pieces, for solo piano
and spoken voice

1. *Ripples*

Long seas.
Long as west is.
Bulging swell.
Lines of small dorsals,
irregular and
loud in this calm.

We're still making way
though the only ripples are
animal movement and
the straight wake of
our cutting keel
in a sea like soup.

A toss of small drops
like sea-trout swirls —
but our track takes us close
to see the fat dorsal and
a distance to the tail's tip
on a basking back.

2. *It goes on down*

A meeting of cloudbanks,
the fronts of systems.
The suggestion of
other islands.

Visible faults
nested white
on the climb and fall
of one volcano.

It goes on down,
clear to deep
but wind shifts fast.
The lee becomes the weather side.

The glass top breaks.
In the turmoil
you have no idea
of depth.

This is a place
where you know that
everything we know
can snap.

3. *Falling figure*

You can pick a rock clean
of dulse or wings

so you jump to the stack,
grab at kelp.
We all take hold
as sea falls away.
The ropes stretch up.

Rips flatten
discordant water
and we're all hunting
our own breath,
stretching and snaring.

The breasts bleed warmth,
strung to your belly
and then it slows.
Every man stops.

All eyes are down
to the one blue bonnet
in the most grey water
but no-one
has fallen yet
out of our number.

We all know
it has still to happen.

4. *Stranding*

Twelve men trust
in an open boat.
Hirta to Boreray —
five nautical miles
in autumn.

Five souls make the jump.
Seven pull away.
They'll be back
in a week or so
as the weather allows.

But later that day
the wind is louder
than the birds.

A wild and bitter night.
The next one's clear.
The sight of flames
comes across
open sea.

One signal fire for each man
who left with a smile.
There are only three fires.
So the stranded men know
the boat was split on stones
like a ling.
Four friends are lost.

A low overlap of stones.
A hat of turf.
They sew skins with bones of birds.

They need to send
their own signal back.
So they cut the living turf
from one side of green,
a mark for each survivor,
a shining square of brown
like a family bible.

If no man is one island
now we know
that no island is
only one.

Come the spring,
a vessel completes the crossing.
First to Hirta then to them.

That five
slide down to
the safe shell.
The same men and boys
and not the same.

5. *St Kilda Fades*

Cooled summits
are close cousins
settled apart.
Their ash has travelled
far enough by now
on the fraying tips
of the Gulf Stream.

Our channels close.
No passage
even for boats.

Before long
all rock is sheer
as the grey spur on
a dogfish back.

Detail diminishes.

Out astern,
all these columns
huddle dense.
Another few miles,
it's all one.

St. Kilda Pieces, with music by David P Graham,
Inventio Musikverlag, Berlin, 2013.

At the Shiants

for GZ

Are there as many kinds of love
as the number of lovers?

Is it like the way
every breeze
that's ever blown
has to be read
second by second
so the sailtrim is
kept in sympathy?

Is it like the way
slow or fast changes
send differing light
to Garbh Eilean
and like the way
the land shouts back
green response?

We're a crew ashore
mad and calm together
chatting like
the 3-knot tideline
balancing the
North and the
Little Minch

but I'm a bit apart now
perched between the tussocks
and familiar
with a bobbing wren.

It's seen me all right
but nothing's a problem
till the weather shifts
with the equinox.

It's the song of Ailean Duinn
pulling bold as today's moon
till the body of the second lover
also lies
on the shingle divide.
It's not so hopeless
– love without
overlapping skin.

harbour insomnia

The hardest thing about sailing is the leaving.

Poems for KC

1. *east side*

sometimes it's nearly enough

a hand across the burn
by mustard ochre
in blazing November

2. *west side*

strange thing is the bit part
of contentment

in this unrelenting
longing

waiting to judge the rise and fall
out where the high stuff folds

cream green
in the crash of Dalmore

3. middle ground

trusting you to see it now –
the line of the hills I know is there

here is the smell of sleet
the dull of a million browns

now and again a wild laugh of light

4. north and south

we might have to meet again
to hear the north and south of it

5. Hemispheres

Like the other guy who didn't need
the rear light on the bike –

'I want to see where I'm going –
I know where I'm coming from.'

Never more settled,
this far so steady but
awake in a wide bed
 – a whiff of tangle.

Your wavelap from
below a dividing line.

6. *If you're ever*

If you're ever on a long bus, guys,
on the long road to Glasgow
travelling with the lingering,
Laphroaig to Highland Park

when a woman on the wide seat
immediately beside you says
you can let your head fall back if you like

and you know that it will fall forever
off a wave
you hadn't even noticed
you were on,
you might as well be easy with it

rather than wonder
for bloody ever
what's the depth of that peppered hair
the olive nature of that skin

and what exactly happens
navigating in neutral
when the speed of the surf
sucks at any
notion of steerage.

7. The nearest you'll see

The nearest you'll see to
water flowing backwards
against the run of slope,
gravity losing support

as the anabatic blast
drives the cliff burn back
up, cloudward

in a rhythm you can't clock
and is irrational
as any sort of unsought want

but rainwater
has a chance
of reaching sea
even if today
you don't see it fall.

My shot again

My shot again
on the rota of the sleepless.
First spell for a while.

Diesel
maybe from under
my short fingernails.

The smell is persistent

as a small drip of blood
spreading in the Dacron weave

of a crisp new sail.

Poems for AP

1. Nothing's fair

Nothing's fair anyway
but I'm wondering
can you hear it,
my inconstant
thunder in a barrel of bones

going
out the door
up the sea-road

swinging a sharp right
over the rips

to find its way
up a geo and ashore
through the chinks

in your sashes
and thresholds?

2. *The evening swell*

The evening swell is difficult
to understand.

You don't know it's there till
the back-bounce.

You look for cause.
See nothing that can

equate with that height.
But you realise the considerable
wavelength when
the black tip of the drying reef
sends signal plumes.

It's like the stories of the three waves,
Ireland to St John's.

Nothing comes from nowhere
but these are from a strange place.

Stranger than the islands, the
ones that only appear
sometimes.

Maybe stranger than terrain
under surfaces.

Your surface is smoother tonight.
Scoured by pumice and black scent.

I smell your smell of want.
It's stitching in my memory but
the pattern halts.

We're off a page.
Two people lie
lonely.

Drifting

prompted by a conversation with Alex Patience

1.

water gone heavy
less of a chop than you'd expect
from recent history of breeze

a surface trace of paraffin
the birds have lost their hurry
rhythms of broaching settle

they might be here or short gone
you might send a wire down
to feel for a tingle

tweak a bakelite dial
tap a battery
nip a connection

sniff for a trace as
the swimmers suck their oxygen
take in glints from the sea's soup

there's a number of fins
even of scales to
a wet hectare
across the given fathoms

the skin of the sea is like nothing
but the skin of the sea
and any skin you're floating on
has her own oil

particular to within
a division in
the gradient of the tide's curve

preparations
can't be hurried

you ease a way in
and you're bound to
your own nets

drifting

2.

waiting is only a half-sleep

just about giving in
to the greatest need

the planet survives
on tensions
she's hung in her orbit
only as sure
as routes of migrations

but when we're up we're up
and into the winching
drops caught in decklights

all moons
as bright as hope

3.

the first blood of the boat
is always a miracle
you expect with doubt

and then you're shaking them
the smell of them and the colour of them
they're never silver

only later
when the heat is chill
and musk is stink

and you have to remember
the weight of number

all the colours that don't have a name
and some of them never will

4.

we're terrier dogs
with the sleekest rats
our hands are fast
as the wings of snipe
and the sound of birds
with the fall of herring
against a longer roll of the Minch

till our shovelling is
another pace again

it's sweet till the spurs
of a ton of grey dogs
dull our dark

the cotton parting
the rasp of sharkskin
hordes of abrasion

our price is losing
with our time
maybe the last will be better

or the corks could be down
with the weight of
a drowned thing

nothing's ever empty but
our last net has nothing to sell
— at least it's whole

5.

the lad's on the pans and
we're burning the diesel
we might just cover it
and the bill for the stores

maybe even that bit more
but stay quiet about it
till the market's done

it's all closed in,
grey as the boiling stew
sloppy with it
she's skewing but steady
the lumpy clouds
are dead doughballs

we've had worse nights
as well as better
the fish are full
and there's only one net
aside for sorting
our decks are shining

when she starts to roll
there's more in the weight
than fuel and water

Sandy Riddle on the sounder
Duncansby Noss Clyth Ness
Kinnaird's still hiding

we'll clock the rest of the marks
check our number in the queue
make a wee shout home

6.

the screw's turning like it
matters
the revs and the rate pretty
constant
if we're spared she'll take us
there

I'm needing wipers on the
glasses
plenty condensing happening
here
needing radar to walk
the wheelhouse

so we'll tick off the blinks till
we're sliding the breakwater
a heaving warp to get us round
the sharp last corner
and we're gliding in

we'll get sold and sorted
before the bairns are in their beds
the morro's for mending

A heron

for RM

there
where
willowglen is bayhead

the silver angler
double

and who cares
if the reflection
is assisted
by artificial light

not the only
restless one
or two
or four
or six
in town

Gensey poems

from The Sked Crew, *a short play devised with Alison Peebles*

1. *Bella's man*

I'm wearing your patterns.
Your threads are holding
my tired bones.
You'll have me home yet
Marybell of Bayhead
when the bugles are sounding
and the decent fisherboys
are rising again
from the ground or the water.

I'm sure there's sea in heaven
and ships and sails and havens.
And strong clean breeze.
We'll be beating for the market
down the zigzag course
knitted in navy
on white water.

A sweet wake
long astern
on all the weight
of British Waters.

All us lost ones
making best course
against the breeze
riding the northerly
into SY.

On to drop the cloth –
the boat's own flax
barked to tan.
Our red wing falls
to black boatskin.

That's what you'll see
when we're home in a glide
on the boat's own way.
Till your long strong hands
are snug about me.

2. *Katag's chiel*

What's fresh cove?
You're seeing it blone.

Foos yer doos?
Aye Peckin.

An the banter's ringin
mair powerful like
an i North Sea itsel
an richt noo I'll tell ye
young teuchter quine
the port o Wick
isna aye a haven.
That breakwater
disnae aye deal
wi a the weight o sea
it's ae place
it's i ony place
the Stevenson chiels
quidna manage
tae build a thing
that wid stan an wark
aginst i weather
ony weather
an since ye ask me
i'll jist need tae tell ye
ye dinna show it
ye canna show it
but when yer boat

is ridin afore it
the surf ahin ye
an yer loons is drunk wi the pride o it
an it looks like ye micht
be the first een en
yer sick tae yer ain hert
at i worry o it
wishin ye were alane
nae ither loon or man
born tae wimmin
tae tak responsibility for
jist yersel an yer sweet black ship
trayin tae haud her
trayin nae tae let the gale
git ahint yer sail cloth
sma canvas tho it be
an judge the wy o it
i safe wy en
i narrow wy
till a they stanes
is shielding ye like
an yer hame or
as near tae hame.
Es'll dae.
A'll be seein that Katag.

3. *Anna's father*

They used to throw ale
to quiet the waves
but, daughter of my own,
you go to the ebb-tide
and drown the gensey.
Watch the wool get heavy.
It'll sink slow.
And don't you worry
I'll find it fine.
And it'll fit
as sure as if I'd been able
to hold out my arms
for the fitting.

I'm seeing you grand
though I only knew you
as the gasp in your mother's breath
at the start of the fullness.

You'll be marching with the bands
the trombones, trumpets
but you'll need to excuse me.
If God can, you can.

I'm so grateful
for the Sound of Shiants
The Little Minch
Sea of the Hebrides
and the rare west wind

that lets you reach
all your destinations.
So I'll be out a bit longer.
It's not greed.
It's appreciation.
Give your mother a hug now
and squeeze your granny's hand.
And there's no need
to be envious
of your brother.
This man loves
both his children.

from *The Sked Crew*, commissioned by Theatre Hebrides,
directed by Alison Peebles with further development
funded by the National Theatre of Scotland.

Poems for VK

1. *There are grains*

There are grains of wild rice with the brown
but they're cultivated
and measured.

If you were here I'd dart across the harbour gale
and chew the fat to negotiate
a pan of langoustines.

Ginger is essential
and I'll stick to green tea.
There's enough going on in my skull
though I'm glad yours has calmed.

The garlic and soy and fermented beans,
the lime to sharpen senses

but I've still so many heads to rest and
I believe I've only seen
two shoulders on you.

2. *Last night*

I dreamed last night there was a tap running,
dripping diesel and it couldn't be stopped
and now the machines whirr

like ventilation ducting
through this empty house.

I'm making electronic love again
and you can't tell if the persona
replying with regularity
has a cold or not.

But I hope your landlord got the plumber out
and your washing machine is spinning
but only the drum.

I think you're troubled
I think there are debt collectors
smoking and waiting
in an office lit by tubes

and there is not a split-screen van
there is not a rally-ready Escort
not even a black cab

nothing with its engine running ready
to take us to the fjord
where our boat is tethered
to a lattice of timbers.

3. *You'll be sleeping*

You'll be sleeping and
I'm sipping fino.

You'll be sleeping and
I'm about to put my sole in a pan.

We'll both be sweating
possibly breathing.

My visitors have left.

The first brought photos of a boat he's bidding for
the second brought a spiced dram of rum
and the third brought
his mother's stories

but you'll be sleeping
or I'd share it all down Facebook.
I'll do that yet
once I've learned how to chat.

4. *There's smoke in the kitchen*

There's smoke in the kitchen
no roast
not squid
not even any kind of frying

not even veg.

It's not tobacco
nothing more fragrant
nothing more pungent.

It's the blue toaster.
Something was trapped.
It was bread once.

It still glows.
The fire alarm didn't go off.
That's worrying

but at 0347
with hail on the ground
not in the kitchen
it'll just have to go
on tomorrow's list
maybe Tuesday's.

There's a warm bed waiting
and I'm not wanting it.
Not sure why

but there's toast and sweet plum jam
and the memory of nightshifts
from more than a dozen years ago.
Out there now
there's cumulonimbus —
airman's nightmare
anvils in the sky

ready to discharge
lightning hail.
And some people out there
are out of their beds
without much choice.

Jets of paraffin
up in the skies.
Fine sprays of diesel
being injected
under waterlines.

Speckle

for LLB

Speckle is fleck
on eggs or breasts or backs.

Your indigo back
has freckles too
and areas that want
a steady pressure
while we talk
or while we wait on
each other's wants.

You brought me black salt
and when it all became implausible,
all these crossings,

I'd steam or lightly roast
grey sole for two
and wait a bit before I ate.

Sometimes a friend might sit with me
and sometimes I could just watch
the tiny darks of rocks
tumble on
a pallid belly.

away and home

The port of arrival is the port of departure.

In Brest

Grey stones of Kersanton.
Ochre from Logonna.
This is the mayor's home,
completed in
1761.

He commissioned the cross on this gable
and a cemetery for the drowned.

But was the ground set aside
to mark lost remains
or did it harbour
only the recovered?

Conversation on Ouessant

Our conversation rang
among the wary blasts
of restricted vessels
nosing fog
outside the marquee.

We drew our own charts,
ink on napkins.
We sipped red bread.
The telling blot
developing from spill.

I know that nobody's
scared of nothing.

There's this story in translation —
how they used to sink
a big bell
down between the reefs
so a signal could be sent
under storm water.
Long before
warning booms
were sustained by gas.

Blue woman, Brittany

Speaking as a navigator
guessing between
a prile of tidal periods
I can understand
in retrospect
now that my hull's been released
everything but
the suddenness.

Even the Mull,
the North Channel,
streams south of Arklow,
St George's Channel,
all allow
a grace of slack.

But I remember
three hours into the passage
warning whorls at the Sound of Shiants
where the blue men hold the ship
and test the eloquence of all aboard.
If they're satisfied, they'll slack their grasp.

But after that trial
even a skipper
has difficulty
responding

to the freedom of a sea
that starts to seem
too large.

El Vigo | Stromness to Stornoway

a winter voyage

to Morven 06 Apr 2010 12:04

rituals of preparation
bending on the mended mainsail
mousing the shackles

to Morven 06 Apr 2010 23:24

a son aboard
last supper of liver
the ropes get thrown at five

to Morven 07 Apr 2010 06:03

Hoy Sound magnifique
in the bounce
– the diesel donkey driving

to Alex 08 Apr 2010 not sent

tang of a bled diesel
we've tacked abeam Kyle of Tongue
we aim to clear Cape Wrath

to Morven 08 Apr 2010 21:12

Tiumpan ducked its head
the breeze is still coming from
where we're going

to Norman 09 Apr 2010 19:11

across the top
forty-two hours of headwinds
— there's easier ways

Crossing the Minch *

Enough light now
to show the shapes of waves

the run of the big hills
betraying
individual traits

as all these particular reds
are streaked by
electrical activity.

You are the goddess
of cumulonimbus
and I could be fascinated again

as the shadow of wit is across your eyes
but I'm also seeing the scud of dark
and know to get all vulnerable sail
to the deck fast and
brace before the sent ice hurts

and then I'll rub my unprotected ears and nose and eyes
and blink at yet another change of sky
and know that continuation would take
the bravery of the solo sailor in
an area of geos and willie-waws
where the notes of pilotage
are sketchy

but I'm on the ferry
and there's snow on an Teallach
and brightness on the Coigeach stone.

It could be time
for an egg-roll.

* The title of a hornpipe (attributed to Donald MacLeod) which
sounds cheerful but is said to have been played by Islanders on
their way to World War II. Many were captured at St Valery and
some were forced on the Long March when the Stalag camps
were evacuated as the Russians advanced.

Broad Bay | Stornoway to Shiants and return

for Rob, a summer expedition

14 Aug 2010 13:11

we're covering ground
that's under a solution
fine air is over
and against us

14 Aug 2010 15:01

our intention looks unlikely
blue is a teased line
mountains all point to it

15 Aug 2010 21:01

the falling ends of islands
or the rising beginnings
they nearly meet

15 Aug 2010 21:14

the moon's a half
sun's taking a dive
blues and reds blacken

17 Aug 2010 08:27

it went dreich
drizzle
two shades below
mi-chailear *
but we were buoyant

* Gaelic word also used in Stornoway-English – a fair bit more
dreich than dreich.

Not crossing the Minch

for CM

If there were no other lives but ours
I'd throw off my ropes
and dart the Minch.

Strange thing how
one single skyline
is a lot of hills.

Tomorrow you'll drive into the middle
and you'll march to one named mass.
The hairs you didn't know you had
will freeze on your face
as near to white as
your hair is close to black.

 I can see it red
on a head that's facing
the other way —
an opposing you
showing how
everything could always be different

except that
the lie of the land
is what it is.

Aboard El Vigo | Stephen Morrison at sea

1. *Loch Leurbost*

Our sloop leans
by a one-sheep-rock,
negotiates with breeze,
nods to the rising tide.

The way a phrase
might not have been said before
is the way our tacking track
probes to the pale,
each side of a chosen line.

There's detail on our fathoms chart —
r for rock and s for sand
jotted down as lead was swung.
The surveys engraved,
in and out of print.

But that fine detail
is not judged necessary now.
Charting is smoothed,
simplified,
like the boundaries
of a country lost
in a larger mass.

So tonight
we'll go close, by sight and feel and
our own untrustworthy memories.
Sure we'll find m for mud
to suck our steel, hold us safe
above the curving soundings,
downwards again till slack.

2. *Cuillin*

This range is
supposed to be red.
Now there's nothing
but haze
at the base of the jagged graph.

You take it on trust,
mountains grow from land
and it's very likely
we're still afloat.
The instruments say so.

I don't believe
our lead keel could glide
on heather stalks or bloom,
not even on honey.

But right now
we could be navigating
this atmosphere

of charged drops,
free of physics
as if we'd been let off the leash,
all three eerie knots
in the fankled cord
eased at last.

There is a tradition, told in the Hebrides, Orkney and Shetland,
that fair winds can be held by two supernatural knots. A third knot
should never be let go but of course it always is.

3. *In Canna harbour*

The gases get up
from a mud bed
to go for surface.

Rippling like sandeels
breaking seaskin
to burst like farts,
fooling our sonar
to display fish
while a proud sky
menstruates

and stark eider
snug in their monochrome layers
celebrate
with comic cries
an orb that's new and dense.

The story goes that the eider was blessed with its share of
down for its diligence in waking to greet the sunrise.

4. *Carvings on Sanda*

Sheep shit
under the span
of sheltering wings
annunciated from stone.

A good shepherd,
like an angel,
will lose sleep
for a weak beast.

The next slab
slants
a few degrees
from plumb.

Coiling bands,
yellow and green,
pronounced in
a brace of snails.

They take on these
colours of lichens
to cheat the thrush.
They've ascended

on sure footings
while we wait
for nearly certain tide
and possible wind.

ACKNOWLEDGEMENTS

These poems could not have been developed without periods
of concentration funded by bursaries from the Scottish Arts
Council and Creative Scotland.

It's not possible to thank all the people who have helped me
make this book but I particularly wish to mention my
previous and present editors:

Anna Rutherford and Kirsten Holst Petersen
    (Dangaroo Press)
Peter Kravitz and Marion Sinclair (Polygon Books)
James Campbell, Robert Alan Jamieson, Murdo Macdonald
    and other editors of *NER* and *The Edinburgh Review*
Graham and Alice Starmore (The Windfall Press)
Alec Finlay (Morning Star Publications, Edinburgh)
Gavin Wallace (The Scottish Arts Council/Creative Scotland)
Gerry Loose, Survivor's Press, Glasgow
Helena Kovaříková, (The British Council, Czech Republic)
Bob Hysek (University of Olomouc/Periplum)
Peter Urpeth (Emergents)
Robyn Marsack (director of the Scottish Poetry Library)
Pete Hay (University of Tasmania)
Sara Hunt and all at Saraband

Alexander Hutchison and Alex Patience advised me on
    Doric nuances.
Many collaborators, across different art forms, have all helped
    shape this work.

This selection includes many poems from previous
   publications.

The author and Saraband are grateful to the publishers of
solo collections, anthologies and periodicals where these have
appeared, often in varying forms. If there are any omissions,
these are an oversight of the author and apologies are
expressed.

SOLO COLLECTIONS

Malin, Hebrides, Minches, Dangaroo Press, Mundelstrup,
   Denmark, 1983
Varying States of Grace, Polygon, Edinburgh, 1987
Buoyage (with Will Maclean), Morning Star Publications, 1993
Providence 2, The Windfall Press, Isle of Lewis, 1994
It's About This, Survivor's Press, Glasgow, 2004
Adrift, Periplum, Olomouc, Czech Republic, 2007
St Kilda Lyrics (music by David P Graham), Inventio
   Musikverlag, Berlin, 2013

ANTHOLOGIES AND EXHIBITION CATALOGUES

Siud an t-eilean, Acair, Stornoway, 1993
Impending Navigation Bright, Morning Star, Edinburgh, 1994
A Talented Digger, creations, cameos and essays in honour of
   Anna Rutherford, editions Rodopi, Amsterdam – Atlanta,
   GA, 1996
Green Waters, edited Alec Finlay, pocketbooks / Polygon,
   Edinburgh, 1998

Present Poets, edited Jenni Calder, National Museums of
   Scotland, 1998
Present Poets 2, edited Jenni Calder, National Museums of
   Scotland, 1999
Inshore, pink and black, An Tobar, Tobermory, 2000
100 Island Poems of Great Britain and Ireland, edited James Knox
   Whittet, Iron Press, Cullercoats, 2005
confluence, Taigh Chearsabhagh, Lochmaddy, 2007
Words Without Borders, edited Bob Hysek, Martina Knápková,
   Mathew Sweney
Festival anthology, Olomouc, Czech Republic, 2007
Islands Without Borders, edited Bob Hysek and Mathew Sweney,
   festival anthology, Olomouc, Czech Republic, 2008
Crossing Alba, curated Laura Hamilton, The Collins Gallery,
   Glasgow, 2010
Caillte, an Lanntair Stornoway, 2011 (assisted by The Hope
   Scott Trust)
These Islands We Sing, edited Kevin MacNeil, Polygon,
   Edinburgh, 2011
Words from an Island, edited Meg Bateman, Skye Reading
   Room, 2013
Oxford Poets, edited Iain Galbraith and Robyn Marsack,
   Manchester, 2013

PERIODICALS WHERE VERSIONS FIRST APPEARED

2 plus 2 (Switzerland), *Cencrastus, Chapman, The Dark Horse,
The Edinburgh Review, Gairfish, The Glasgow Magazine, London
Magazine, Kunapipi* (Denmark), *New Edinburgh Review, Nomad,
Northwords, Northwords Now, Poetry Australia, Poetry Canada Review,*

*Poetry Salzburg Review, Scotia Rampant, The Scottish
Mountaineering Club Journal, Poetry Scotland, Poetry Wales,
Stand, Strata*

Some of the poems were broadcast on BBC Radio Scotland
and another was selected by Jon Silkin for *Poetry Now*
(BBC Radio 3).

AUTHOR'S NOTE

Spellings and styles of boat names, place-names of Gaelic
origin, foreign language words, and other similar choices are
those adopted by the author.

Any inconsistencies are part of his attempt to reflect daily
usage, as he is aware of it.

A NOTE ON THE TYPE

maritime is set in Eric Gill's classic serif Perpetua in
Monotype's Pro version, which adds small caps and other
glyphs to his famous original. The section openings and
some subheadings are set in Helvetica Neue 45 Light.